5 FINGER
CHRISTMAS FUN

11 Delightful Melodies Arranged for Piano with Optional Duet Accompaniments

TOM GEROU

Foreword

These Christmas favorites have been arranged in traditional five-finger style, with the melody split between the left and right hands, and without key signatures in the solo part. Starting hand positions are illustrated above each piece. Fingerings that are outside of the noted five-finger positions and those indicating a shift in hand position are circled ① for easy identification. Dotted quarter notes, triplets and sixteenth notes have been avoided. Leader lines in lyrics are omitted to avoid clutter. All of the melodic arrangements have optional duet accompaniments created to achieve a fuller, richer musical experience.

Contents

All I Want for Christmas Is My Two Front Teeth. 8
Deck the Halls. 14
Frosty the Snowman 30
Jingle Bell Rock 26
Jingle Bells 11
Jolly Old Saint Nicholas 4
A Marshmallow World. 16
O Christmas Tree 20
Santa Claus Is Comin' to Town 22
Toyland 6
Up on the Housetop. 2

Alfred

D1509431

ISBN-10: 0-7390-5551-8
ISBN-13: 978-0-7390-5551-9

Up on the Housetop

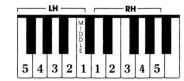

Music by Benjamin Hanby
Arr. by Tom Gerou

Moderate swing tempo

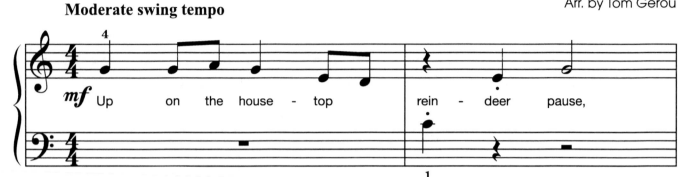

Up on the house - top rein - deer pause,

out jumps good old San - ta Claus. Down through the chim - ney with

Optional Duet Accompaniment (Play solo part 1 octave higher than written.)

Moderate swing tempo

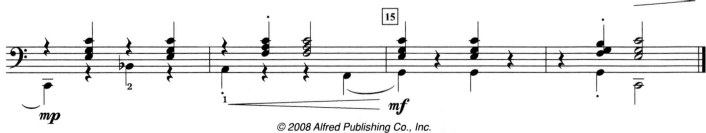

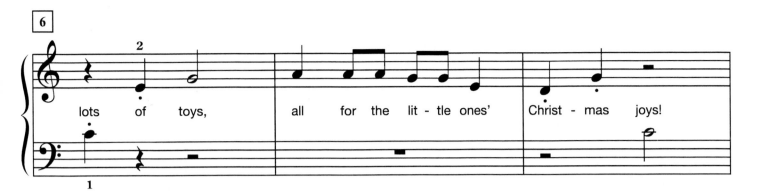

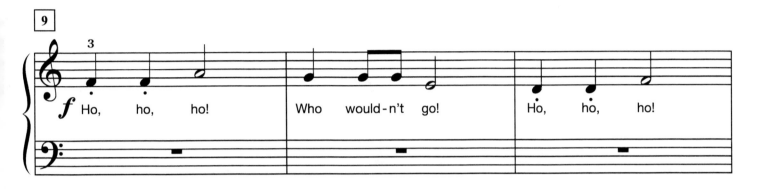

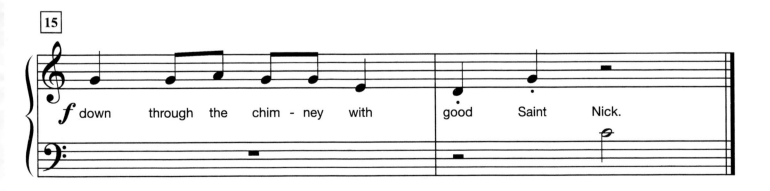

Jolly Old Saint Nicholas

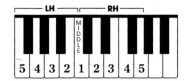

Traditional
Arr. by Tom Gerou

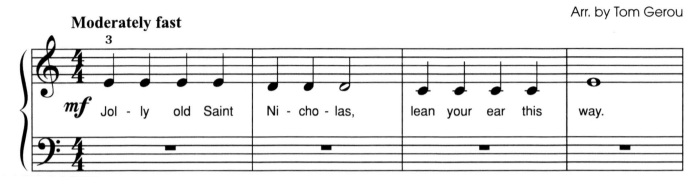

Moderately fast

Jol - ly old Saint Ni - cho - las, lean your ear this way.

Don't you tell a sin - gle soul what I'm going to say. Christ - mas Eve is

Optional Duet Accompaniment (Play solo part 1 octave higher than written.)

com - ing soon, now, you dear old man, whis - per what you'll

3

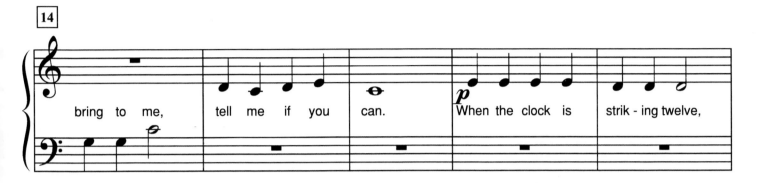

bring to me, tell me if you can. When the clock is strik - ing twelve,

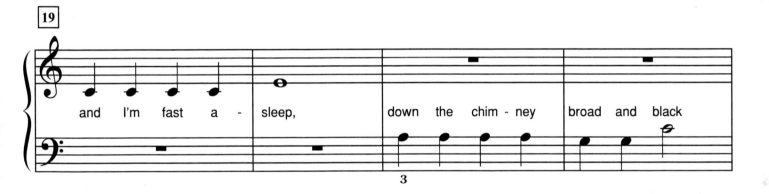

and I'm fast a - sleep, down the chim - ney broad and black

3

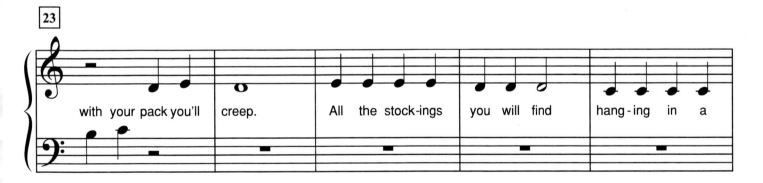

with your pack you'll creep. All the stock-ings you will find hang - ing in a

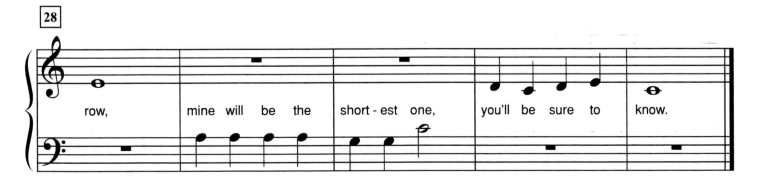

row, mine will be the short - est one, you'll be sure to know.

Toyland
(Babes in Toyland)

Words by Glen MacDonough
Music by Victor Herbert

Arr. Tom Gerou

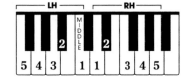

Moderate waltz tempo

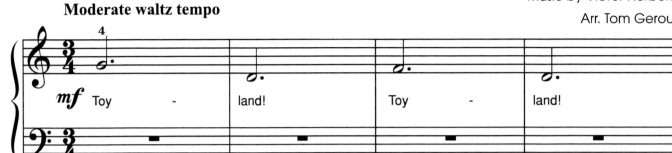

mf Toy - land! Toy - land!

Lit - tle girl and boy land.

Optional Duet Accompaniment (Play solo part 1 octave higher than written.)

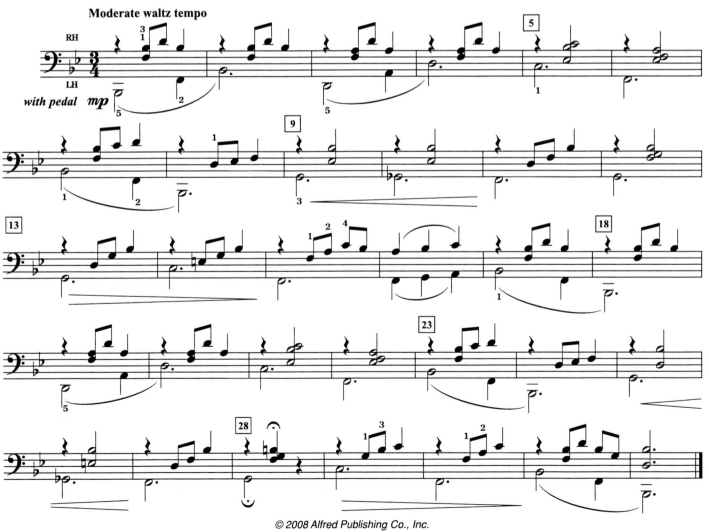

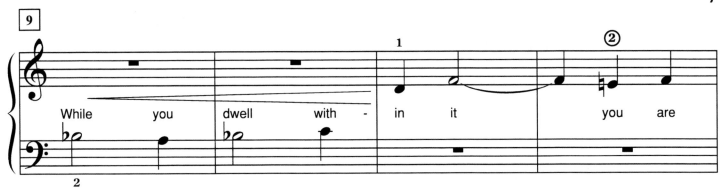

While you dwell with - in it you are

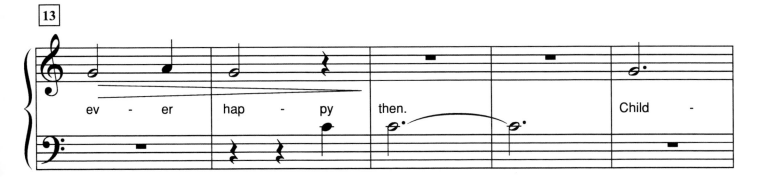

ev - er hap - py then. Child -

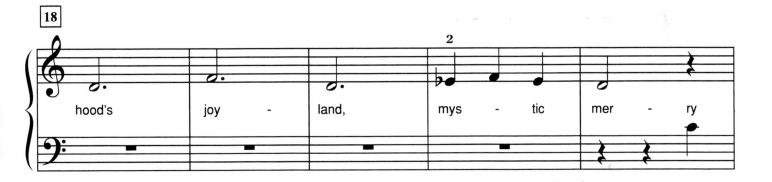

hood's joy - land, mys - tic mer - ry

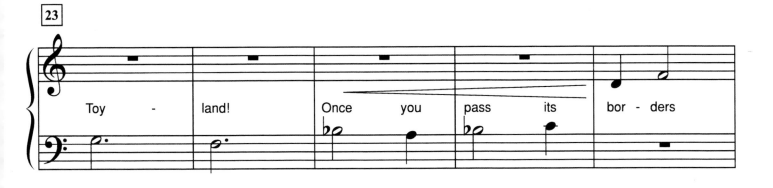

Toy - land! Once you pass its bor - ders

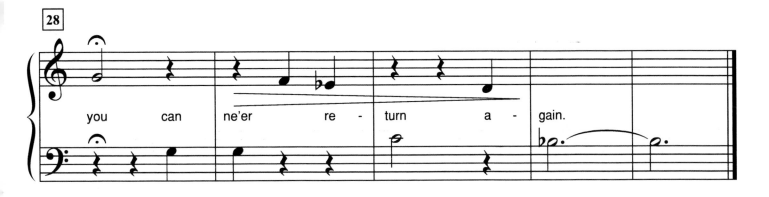

you can ne'er re - turn a - gain.

All I Want for Christmas Is My Two Front Teeth

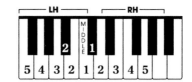

Words and Music by Don Gardner

Arr. by Tom Gerou

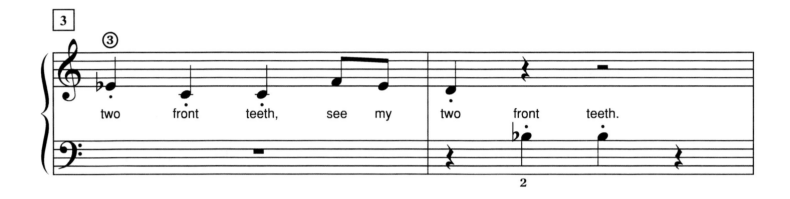

Moderately

mf All I want for Chirst-mas is my two front teeth, my

two front teeth, see my two front teeth.

Optional Duet Accompaniment (Play solo part 1 octave higher than written.)

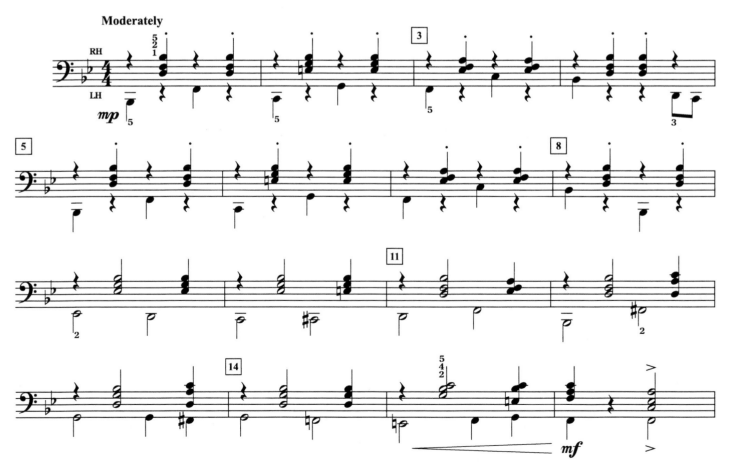

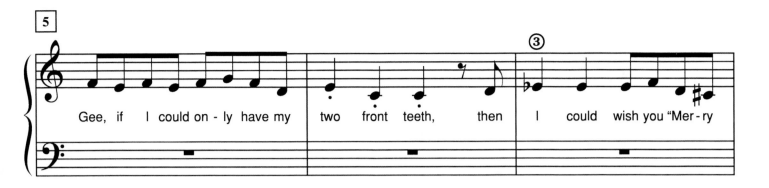

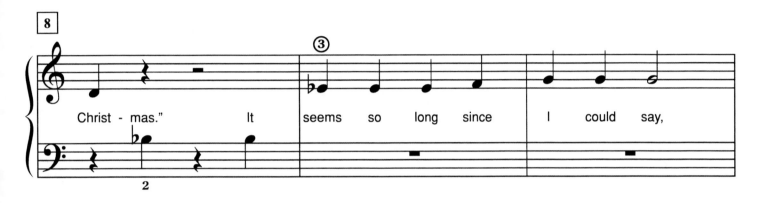

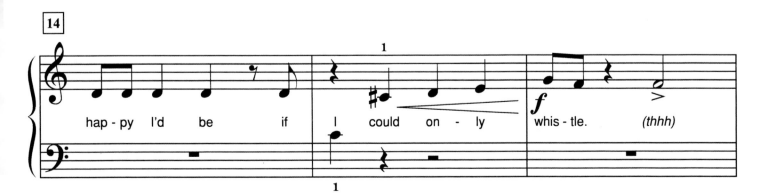

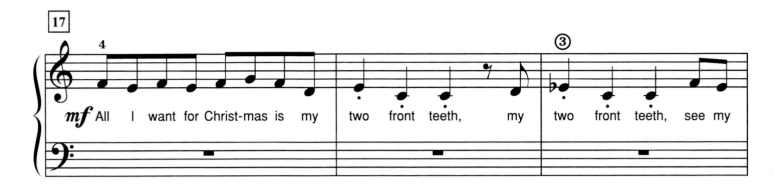

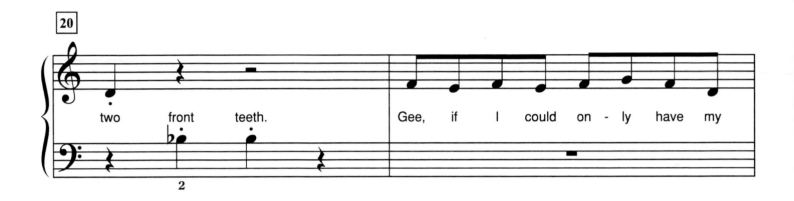

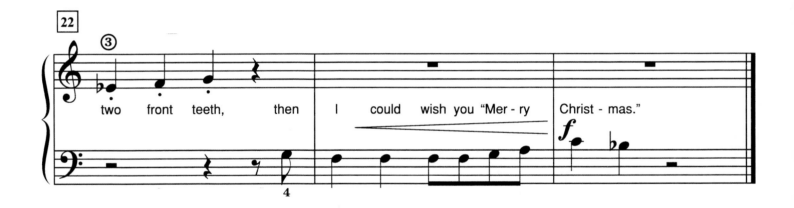

(duet continued)

Jingle Bells

Music by James Pierpoint
Arr. by Tom Gerou

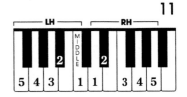

Brightly

Dash - ing through the snow in a one - horse o - pen sleigh,

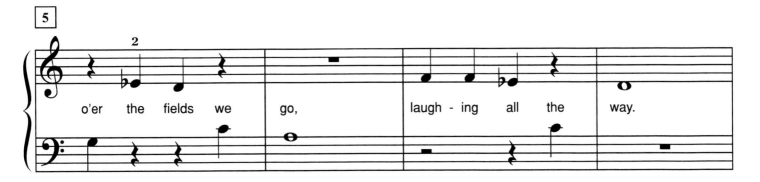

o'er the fields we go, laugh - ing all the way.

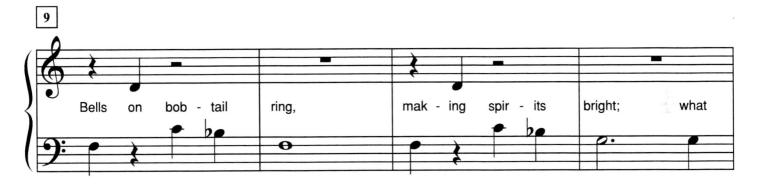

Bells on bob - tail ring, mak - ing spir - its bright; what

Optional Duet Accompaniment (Play solo part 1 octave higher than written.)

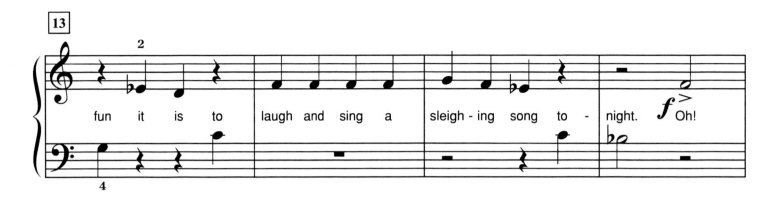

fun   it   is   to   laugh and sing   a   sleigh - ing song to - night. *f* Oh!

(duet continued)

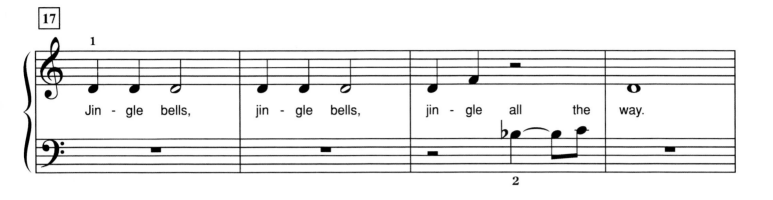

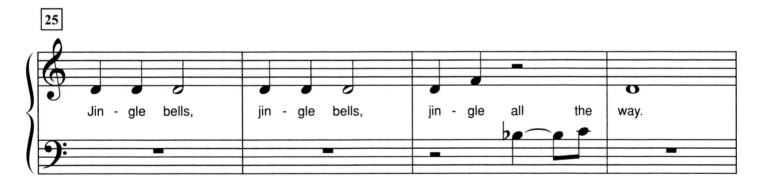

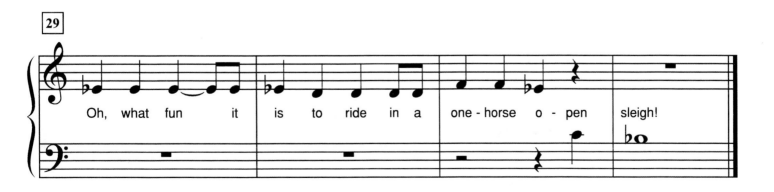

Deck the Halls

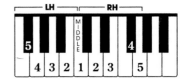

Traditional
Arr. by Tom Gerou

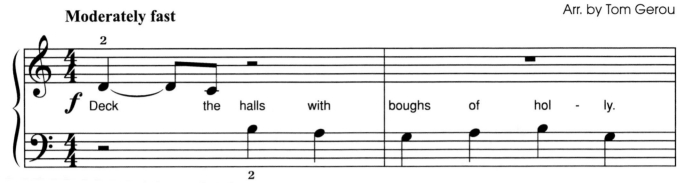

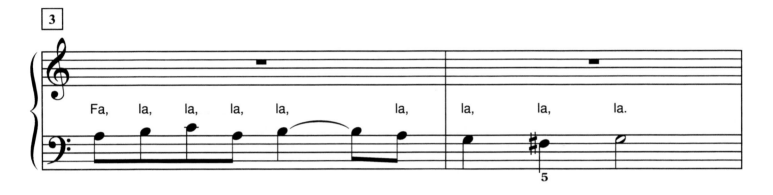

Optional Duet Accompaniment (Play solo part 1 octave higher than written.)

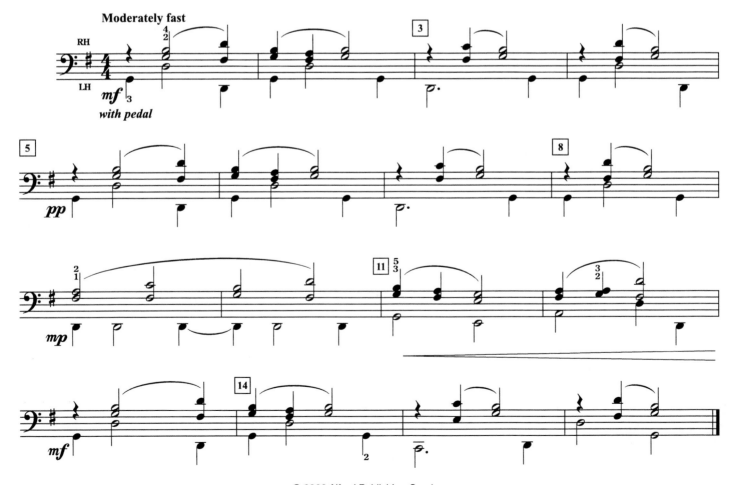

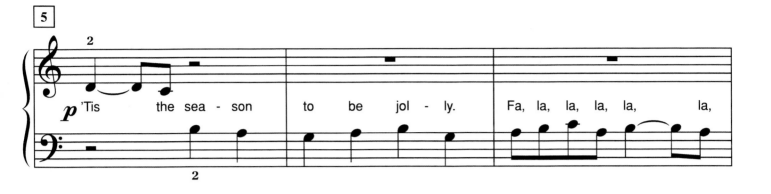

A Marshmallow World

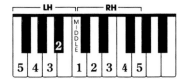

Words by Carl Sigman
Music by Peter De Rose

Arr. by Tom Gerou

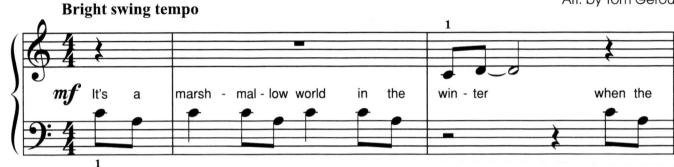

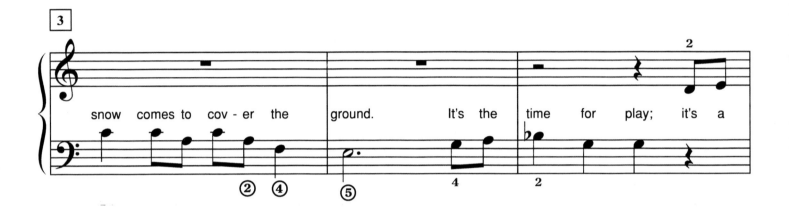

Optional Duet Accompaniment (Play solo part 1 octave higher than written.)

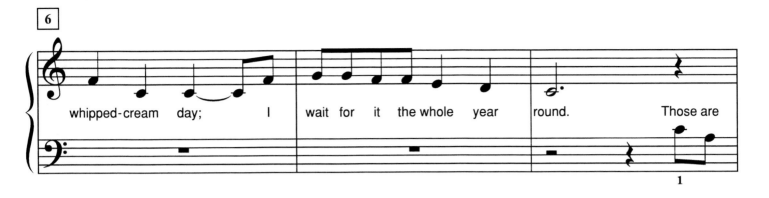

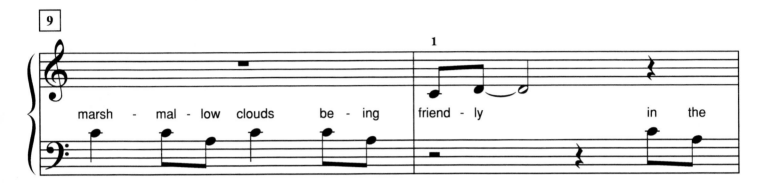

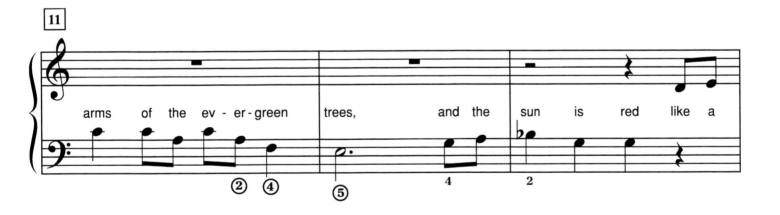

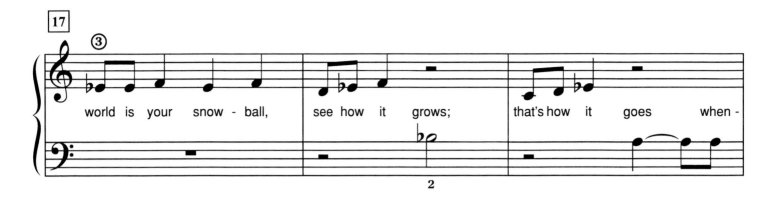

(duet continued)

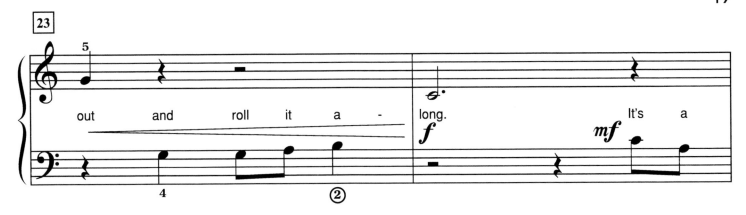

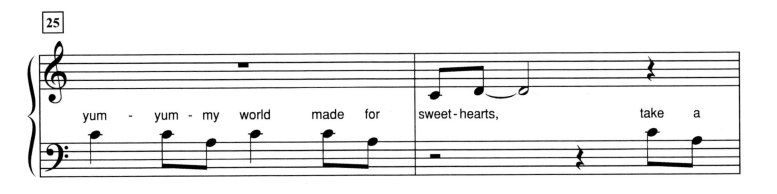

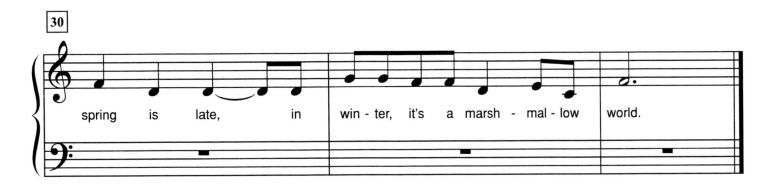

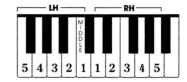

O Christmas Tree

Traditional

Arr. by Tom Gerou

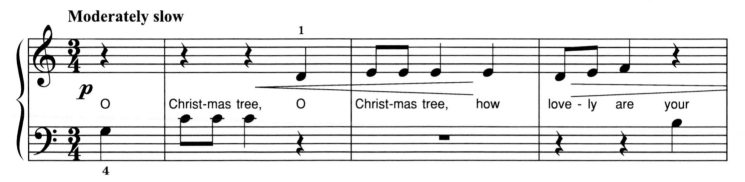

Moderately slow

O Christ-mas tree, O Christ-mas tree, how love - ly are your

Optional Duet Accompaniment (Play solo part 1 octave higher than written.)

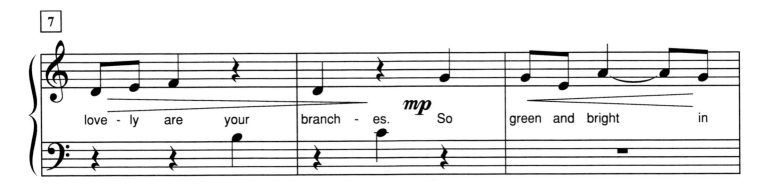

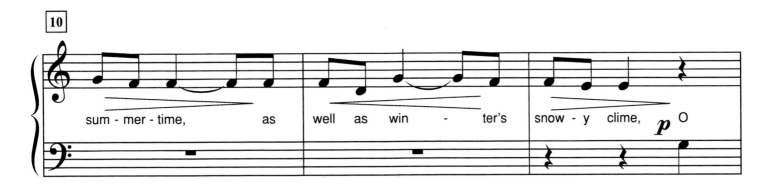

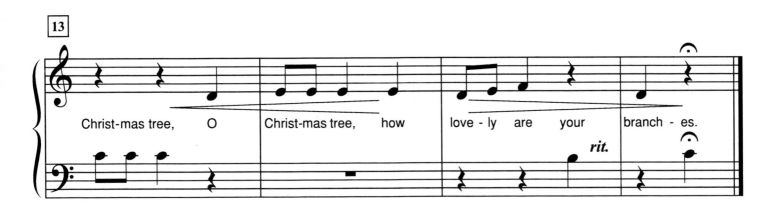

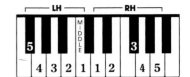

Santa Claus Is Comin' to Town

Music by J. Fred Coots
Arr. by Tom Gerou

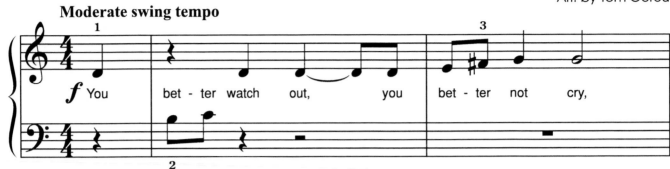

You bet-ter watch out, you bet-ter not cry,

bet-ter not pout, I'm tell-in' you why: San-ta Claus is

Optional Duet Accompaniment (Play solo part 1 octave higher than written.)

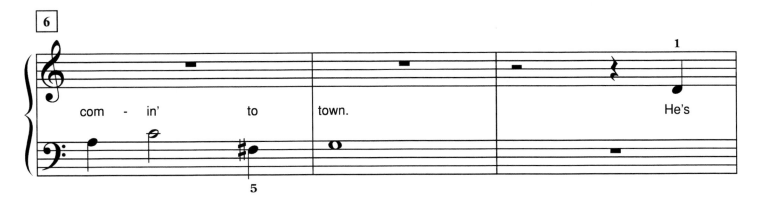

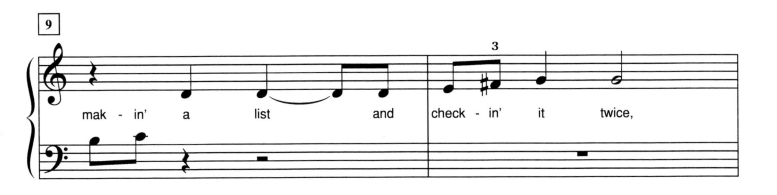

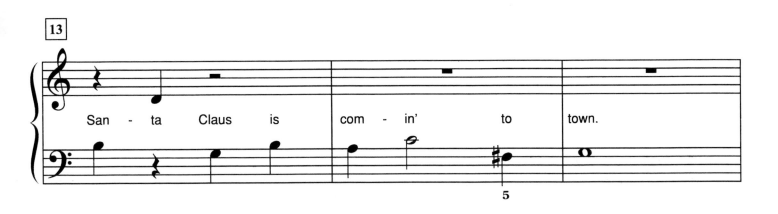

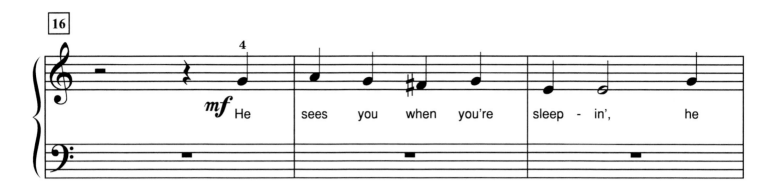

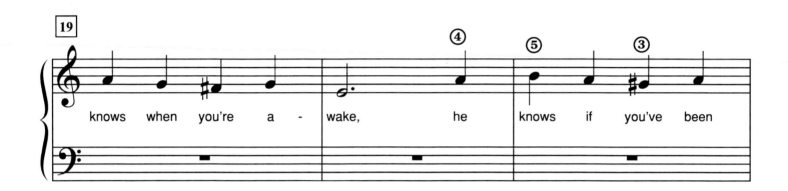

(duet continued)

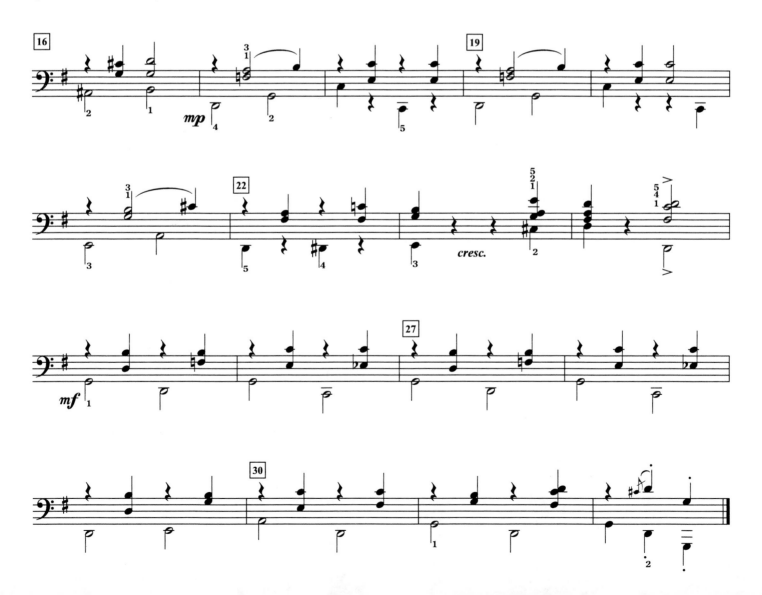

bad or good so be good for good - ness sake! _f_ Oh, you

bet - ter watch out, you bet - ter not cry,

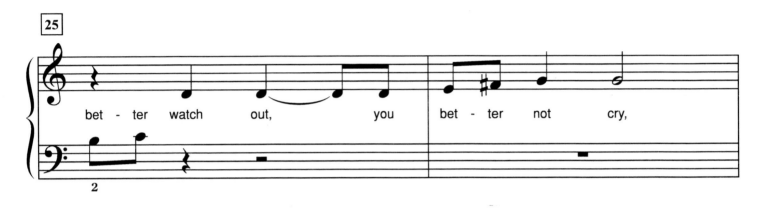

bet - ter not pout, I'm tell - in' you why:

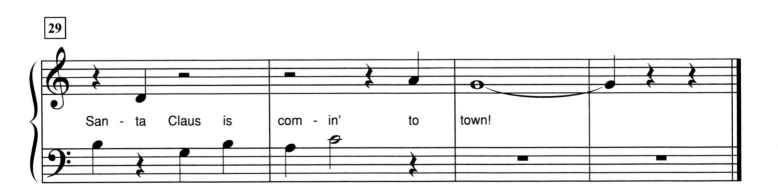

San - ta Claus is com - in' to town!

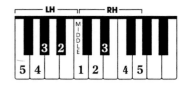

Jingle Bell Rock

Words and Music by Joe Beal and Jim Boothe

Arr. by Tom Gerou

Moderate swing tempo

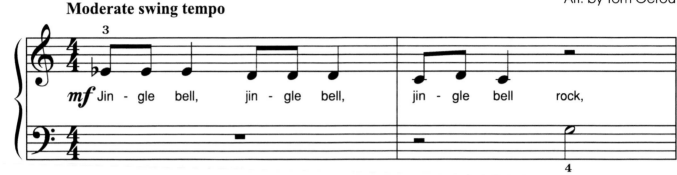

Jin - gle bell, jin - gle bell, jin - gle bell rock,

jin - gle bells swing and jin - gle bells ring. Snow-in' and blow-in' up

Optional Duet Accompaniment (Play solo part 1 octave higher than written.)

Moderate swing tempo

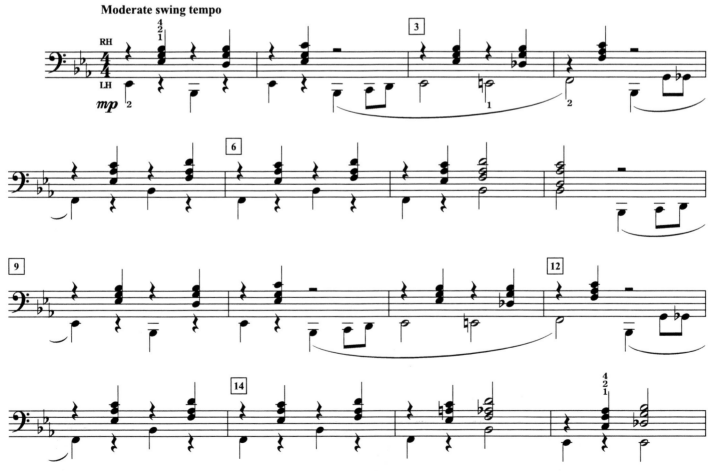

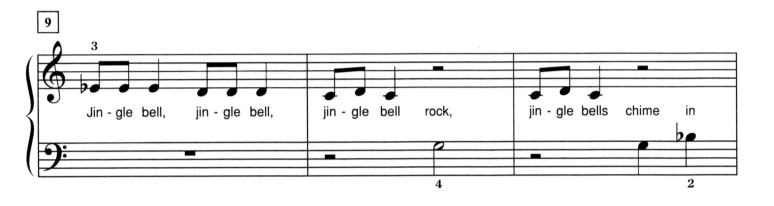

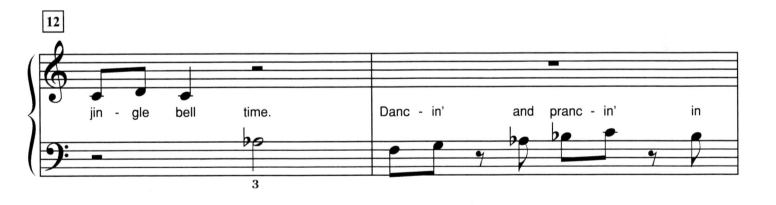

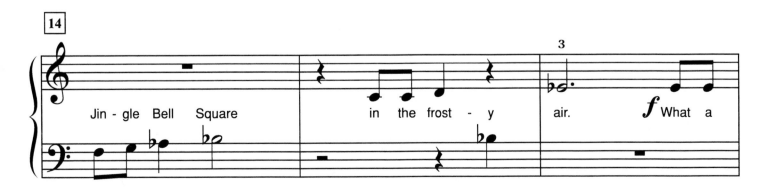

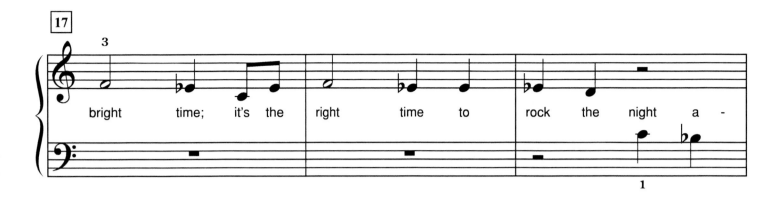

(duet continued)

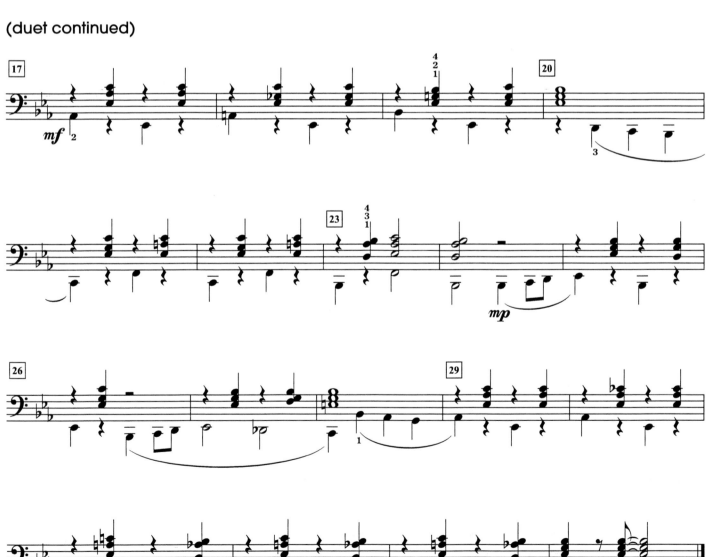

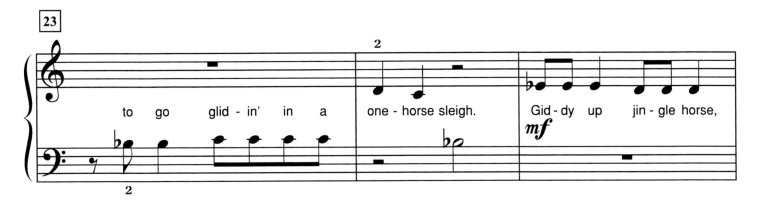

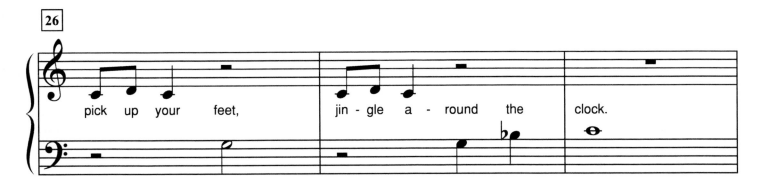

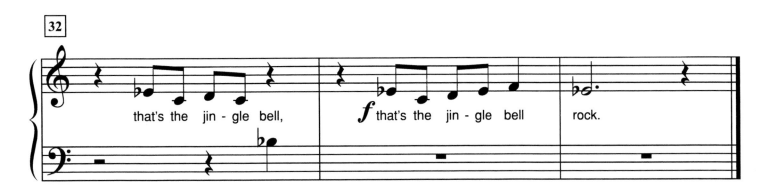

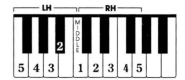

Frosty the Snowman

Words and Music by Steve Nelson and Jack Rollins

Arr. by Tom Gerou

Frost - y, the snow - man was a jol - ly hap - py
Frost - y, the snow - man knew the sun was hot that

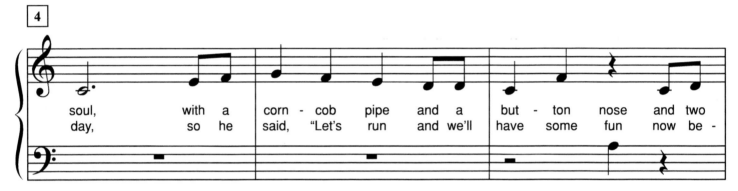

soul, with a corn - cob pipe and a but - ton nose and two
day, so he said, "Let's run and we'll have some fun now be -

Optional Duet Accompaniment (Play solo part 1 octave higher than written.)

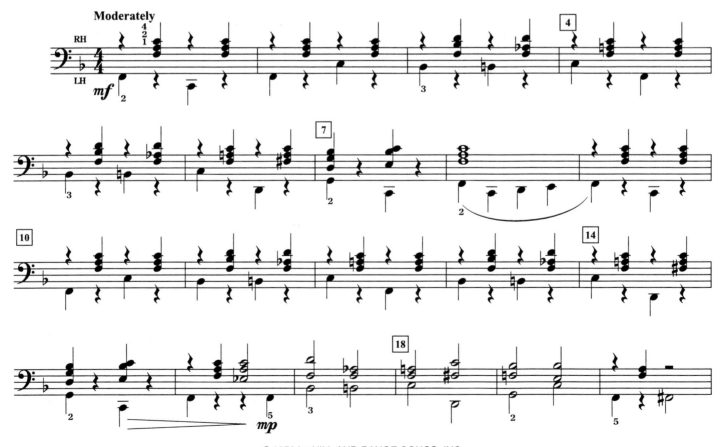

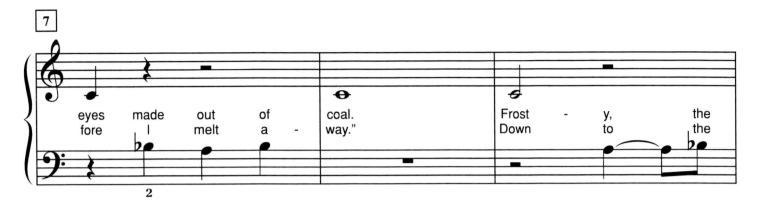

eyes made out of coal.
Frost - y, the

fore I melt a - way."
Down to the

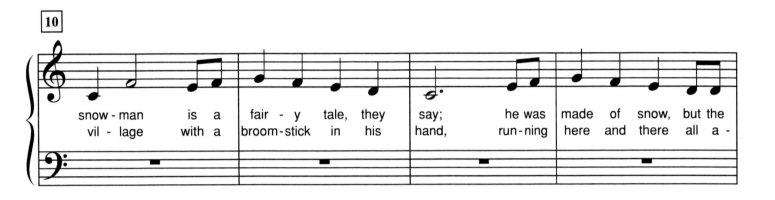

snow - man is a fair - y tale, they say; he was made of snow, but the

vil - lage with a broom-stick in his hand, run - ning here and there all a -

chil - dren know how he came to life one day. **mf** There must have been some

round the square, say-in', "Catch me if you can." He led them down the

mag - ic in that old silk hat they found, for

streets of town right to the traf - fic cop, and he

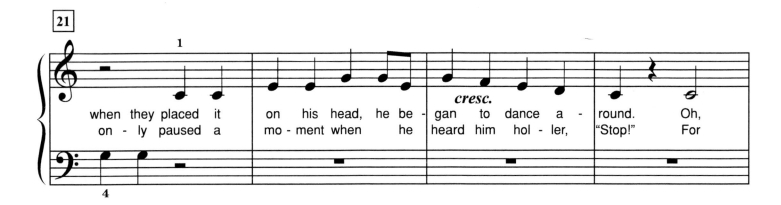

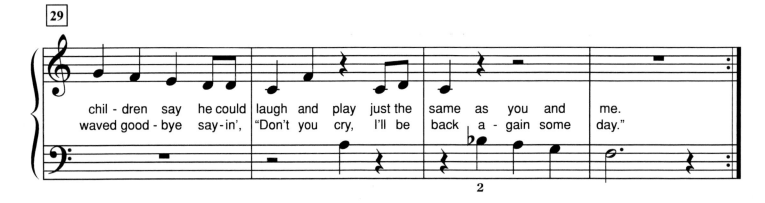

(duet continued)